·95

SUPER-CHARGED!

POWER BOAT RACING

BY

T. J. Andersen

PUBLISHED BY

CRESTWOOD HOUSE

Mankato, MN, U.S.A.

CIP

LIBRARY OF CONGRESS CATALOGING IN PUBLICATION DATA

Andersen, T. J.
   Power boat racing.
   (Super-charged!)
   SUMMARY: Describes the power boats used for racing, their equipment, the categories of racing, aspects of safety, and the forms of competition.
   1. Motorboat racing — Juvenile literature. [1. Motorboat racing]   I. Title.
GV835.9.A53   1988   797.1'4   87-30502
ISBN 0-89686-359-X

International standard Book Number 0-89686-359-X	Library of Congress Catalog Card Number: 87-30502

CREDITS

Cover: FPG International (Ron Whitby)
Popeyes Fried Chicken Offshore Racing Team: 35, 36
Hydroplanes, Inc.: 27; (Michael Moore) 12; (Paul Kemel) 38; (Grant Ramaley) 39
American Eagle Marine: 37
Bob Black & Company: 40
Bettmann News Photos: 18
Third Coast Stock Source: (John M. Touscany) 16-17, 32-33; (Buck Miller) 24-25
FPG International: (Ron Whitby) 7, 10, 28-29; (Philip Wallick) 8-9; (Zimmerman) 11, 26, 30-31, 44
Focus West: (Robert Beck) 4, 20-21; (Robert Brown) 15, 19, 22-23; (S. Kendall) 42

Acknowledgements to Gloria Urbin, American Power Boat Association, and Fred Farley, International Unlimited Hydroplane Hall of Fame and Museum.

Produced by Carnival Enterprises.

CRESTWOOD HOUSE

Box 3427, Mankato, MN, U.S.A. 56002

TABLE OF CONTENTS

THE CHALLENGE OF BOAT RACING

Imagine racing across the water at very high speeds. The front of your boat is completely out of the water, and you're hitting the waves so fast that half the time your whole boat is in the air. Behind you is an arc of water—a roostertail almost 100 yards (91 meters) long.

The challenge of boat racing is to complete the course faster than your competitors. Sound easy? As you round each buoy that marks the course, you are faced with decisions. You don't want to give up too much speed, but if you go too fast, you may lose control of the boat. At any time, too much air could get under your boat and cause it to flip over. You've seen this happen to your competitors. If you hit or miss the buoy, you will be penalized by having to race an extra lap. You don't want to do that—you're in this race to win!

People who race boats love speed. Many high-speed boat racers have also driven race cars or flown airplanes. For everyone who participates in this sport, high-speed boat racing provides thrills beyond compare.

Power boats are fast!

BEGINNINGS

Motor boat racing dates back to the invention of motor boats. In the late 1800's, a new kind of boat appeared on Long Island Sound, the body of water between New York and Connecticut. These boats had been fitted with combustion (fuel-burning) engines.

Soon their owners began to race with each other. By 1902, enough people were interested in boat racing that rules and regulations were needed. Because the early propeller-driven boats were built by their owners rather than a factory, every boat was different and had different capabilities. Some means of handicapping (equalizing the opportunity for all boats) had to be created.

In 1903, the American Power Boat Association (APBA) was formed to fill this need. The APBA set up racing divisions and wrote a rule book. Although categories, classes, and divisions have changed many times since then, the APBA is still the governing body for boat racing in the United States.

MODERN POWER BOAT RACING

Today over 4,000 racing boats and 8,000 people participate in the sport of power boat racing.

Boat races are held all across North America and attract big crowds.

Throughout the year, boat races are held all across North America—on city lakes and rivers, on the Great Lakes, and along the Atlantic and Pacific coastlines. In all, nearly 400 APBA-approved races take place each year.

A power boat's inboard motors cannot be seen or removed.

MOTORS

Without motors, of course, power boat racing would not exist! Manufacturers make different types of motors, which vary according to how they are attached to the boat. Power, size, and fuel type are all factors in choosing a motor.

The amount of horsepower (hp) an engine should

have is determined by the kind and size of boat it will be used with. Big boats can have powerful engines; on small boats, the horsepower is limited. The more horsepower an engine has, the more fuel it uses.

Inboard motors are built into a boat in much the same way that a car's engine is part of a car. They aren't visible, and they aren't meant to be removed.

Outboard motors are mounted on the boat after it

One outboard motor usually supplies enough power to the racing boat...

is made. They can be detached, although some of today's engines are so heavy that even a professional weightlifter could not budge them.

Some boats have more than one motor. A big boat might have either one 300-hp motor or dual (two) 150-hp motors. Dual motors reduce the chances of becoming stranded in the water. If one engine quits working, the other can keep the boat moving. But a two-motor system has drawbacks. Just by trailing in

...but sometimes three motors are best!

the water, a motor's propeller creates a certain amount of resistance, or drag. Two motors increase this underwater drag. For example, a boat with two 150-hp engines will not move quite as fast as a boat with a single 300-hp engine.

Propeller motors also affect the way a boat is steered. As the propeller turns, it produces torque, or movement in the opposite direction. A propeller turning clockwise will push the boat forward and also slightly to the left. To compensate for this torque, the driver must steer the boat slightly to the right.

Some dual systems are now built with counter rotation. The starboard (right) propeller turns clockwise, while the port (left) propeller turns counterclockwise. In this way, each cancels out the torque produced by the other, and the boat is propelled directly forward.

The enclosed cockpit of this power boat provides extra protection for the driver.

The new large engines have been designed so that they are easier to use and to maintain. One important option is power steering. For a racer steering a 500-pound (226-kilogram) motor in a race where every second counts, power steering is a must!

Another convenience is oil injection. Owners once had to dump a quart of oil into the gas tank every now and then to create the proper oil and gas mixture. With oil injection, the engine automatically takes in oil from a holding tank as it needs it.

For years, the best-known manufacturers of boat engines have been Evinrude, Johnson, and Mercury. Recently, though, Japanese manufacturers introduced several new brands into the American market. Today if you walk down to a marina, you're likely to see outboard motors with names like Suzuki, Yamaha, Honda, Nissan, and Tohatsu in addition to the familiar American names.

SPECIAL ENGINES

Standard engines aren't used in all racing events, however. Some racing categories and classes allow engines that have been modified, or changed. Still others allow engines that were designed for other vehicles, such as cars or airplanes.

In the Modified Outboard category, boats must use stock marine engines manufactured in the United

States. Legal changes to the engine include removing and replacing parts and adding specially built exhaust systems. The resulting motor must still meet standard specifications and run on ordinary gasoline and oil.

Many of the boats that compete in the Inboard, PRO Outboard, Offshore, and Drag categories have customized engines made by such companies as Ford, Chevrolet, or Toyota. Depending on the division and class, Inboard Endurance crafts can use engines manufactured for standard production car, boat, or truck use.

The most powerful engines in boat racing are found in the Unlimited category. Since the end of World War II when Unlimited racing began, two engines have dominated the field: the Allison engine, used in the American P38 fighter plane, and the Rolls Royce Merlin, used in the British Spitfire, also a fighter plane. Both engines are capable of delivering between 2,000 and 2,500 hp. Until just a few years ago, almost all the boats in the Unlimited category were powered by these surplus World War II engines.

In 1984, Unlimited racing was changed forever by the introduction of turbine engines—jet engines taken out of helicopters. The standing record for a lap in an Unlimited is 153.061 miles per hour (mph) or 246 kilometers per hour (km/h), set in 1984 by Chip Hanauer with a special turbine engine called

The most powerful racing boats enter contests in the Unlimited category.

the L-11.

In 1986, the APBA ruled out the 3,600-hp L-11. There was simply no contest between it and the less-powerful piston engines. The L-7, with 2,650 hp, is now the top turbine engine allowed in the Unlimited category. All speed records since 1984 have been set by turbine-powered boats.

A power boat race determines which boat is the fastest!

V-bottoms are sleek and fast.

POWER BOAT HULLS

Just as you can't have a power boat without a motor, you can't have a boat without a hull. The hull is, after all, the body of the boat!

Power boat hulls can be made of fiberglass, wood, or metal. The shape of the hull, its length, and its width all affect the speed and handling of the boat. Runabouts are flatbottom boats. V-bottoms, as their

18

Some power boats have sponsons attached to the hull to avoid tipping over while racing.

name implies, have a bottom that forms a V. One kind of V-bottom is called a Deep-Vee.

Another hull design is the tunnel, a combination hydroplane and flatbottom made of fiberglass. Tunnel boats are both fast and stable.

Hydroplanes have a unique hull design. The hulls are usually built of honeycomb aluminum, which is strong but lightweight. Sponsons, or pontoon-like floats, are attached to either side of the hull. These give the boat added stability. When the boat is

In a cabover design, the engine is located behind the driver.

skimming along at racing speed, the sponsons and the propeller are the only parts touching the water (these areas that make contact with the water are called the planing surface).

One design feature of hydroplanes—the cabover—has become quite popular since it first appeared more than 20 years ago. In the cabover

design, the engine is mounted in the rear and the driver sits in front of it, almost in the middle of the boat. In the standard hydroplane hull, the driver sits behind the engine. The cabover design is safer and allows the boat to take corners smoothly. Since 1978, all new boats in the Unlimited class have used cabover hulls.

Power boat drivers wear helmets and life jackets for protection in case of an accident.

Hydroplanes look like small jet planes.

RACING CATEGORIES

Because of the many different kinds of boats and motors in the sport of boat racing, there are hundreds of racing classes. These classes are grouped into nine racing categories. The placement of the boat's engine (inboard or outboard) and the shape of its hull (flat or round) decide the category of a racing boat.

Unlimited Hydroplane racing is probably the most spectacular of all the categories. The hydroplanes in this category look like small jet planes. They have streamlined shapes and incredibly powerful inboard engines. Often called "thunderboats," they are powered by massive aircraft piston or turbine engines. The drivers, who must be highly skilled to handle these machines, compete at speeds of up to

The driver, throttleman, and navigator work together to race the power boat to the finish line.

200 mph (321 km/h).

Offshore racing combines speed, navigation, and endurance. Teams of three racers—driver, throttleman, and navigator—work together to race through anywhere from 100 to 200 miles (160 to 321 kilometers) of open waters. The 30- to 50-foot (9- to 15-meter) catamarans or Deep-Vees are powered by multiple inboard or outboard engines. Competitors are pitted against rough seas and tough opponents. Some have called Offshore racing the ultimate test of endurance.

Drag boat racing pits one boat against another for a quarter mile (.4 kilometer) of excitement at speeds over 200 mph (321 km/h)! Competition in this category includes both professional and amateur events.

Before every race, the crew carefully inspects their boat.

Concentration is needed to steer a small power boat through choppy water.

OUTBOARD CATEGORIES

Stock Outboard racing is often the category for beginners. Because the outboard engines must be stock (as produced by the factory, and not altered), the equipment for this category is pretty inexpensive.

Racers of all ages can participate. The classes within this category depend on the make and horsepower of the engines. No boat has an advantage over another because of engine size. The outcome of the race depends more on fine-tuning and driving ability. Average racing speeds range from 40 to 60 mph (64

A power boat skims along the water on its way to the finish line.

to 96 km/h).

Modified Outboard racing is often the next step for those who have been racing in the Stock Outboard category. Here stock engines undergo complete changes to deliver greater speed and performance. These "souped-up" engines are fitted on hydros and runabouts. Competitors race at speeds of 60 to 90 mph (96 to 144 km/h).

Professional Outboard racing, or PRO Outboard, offers competitors the greatest freedom in altering

their equipment. Sophisticated custom-built engines burn special fuels that contain alcohol. Boats in this category reach speeds of over 100 mph (160 km/h).

Outboard Performance Craft racing offers competition for many kinds of boat styles and engines. A common style in this category is the tunnel boat, a combination hydroplane and flatbottom that is both fast and stable. Boats are from 12 to 18 feet (3 to 5 meters) long and agile enough to make a quick turn at 140 mph (225 km/h)!

It's one power boat against another in drag boat racing.

OTHER CATEGORIES

Inboard racing is a category that includes something for everyone. Hydroplanes and flatbottoms compete in a variety of classes ranging from the small beginner's stock engine to the super-powered Grand Prix boats. Equipment varies from pure stock—boats straight off the dealer's lot—to completely customized. Competitors race in a circle, hitting speeds ranging from 70 to 150 mph (112 to 241 km/h).

Inboard Endurance racing is the sport's "distance" event. These marathon races test drivers and their equipment against a set time limit or a set distance. Drivers compete by doing laps around a closed course of one to three miles (1.5 to 4 kilometers).

A new division, *Special Events,* allows anyone on any kind of motorized water craft to compete. This division contains classes for Wetbikes, Surf Jets, and other kinds of craft. Competitors in these classes have the chance to set world records and compete for national championships.

THE DRIVERS

Winning races and setting records is a team effort. Drivers, navigators, and throttlemen are in the spotlight during an exciting race, but their

The Popeye Racing Team's 50-foot superboat.

performance depends on owners, builders, designers, and engineers. Many owners and builders are former drivers. In many classes, the driver is the owner.

Al Copeland and his son, Al, Jr., have been both teammates and friendly rivals. In the 1986 world championship races at Key West, Florida, both competed in the Offshore open class. The senior Al drove *Popeyes 1,* with 2,800 hp, and Al, Jr., drove *Popeyes/Diet Coke 10,* with three 700-hp inboards.

This 35-foot catamaran is another part of the Popeye Racing Team.

The senior Al beat his son to the finish line by just one second to win the 1986 World Cup!

The Copelands aren't the only father-son pair to be involved in Offshore racing. Tom Gentry and his son, Norm, team up as driver and navigator in the *Turbo Eagle.* The Gentrys build their own engines and props. John D'Elias and his son, J.D., both race in different Offshore classes. John owns and drives *Special Edition,* while J.D. is the throttleman for *Breakaway.*

The **Turbo Eagle** is the Gentry's winning power boat.

*Bernie Little shows off **Miss Budweiser's** trophy.*

*It's always fun to watch the **Miss Budweiser** race!*

In the Unlimited category, *Miss Budweiser* has been a real champion. Driven by Jim Kropfeld, this $1 million hydroplane is outfitted with an L-7 turbine engine and has no trouble taking laps at speeds of over 150 mph (241 km/h)! Bernie Little, *Miss Budweiser's* owner, has owned and sponsored Unlimited racing boats since 1963. His boats have won one World Championship, six National High Point Championships, and five Gold Cups.

Driver Betty Cook races her powerful boat.

Another frequent winner in the Unlimited category is Chip Hanauer. He drives *Miller American,* owned by Frances Muncey. The Muncey family has long been active in power boat racing. Bill Muncey, Frances's husband, was an owner/driver until his death in 1981. Muncey has been called the "winningest" driver ever and still holds the record for having won more races than anyone else. He is

the only person to have won the APBA Gold Cup—
the top prize in the Unlimited class—eight times!

BOAT RACING SAFETY

Despite many safety precautions, accidents happen from time to time. Some accidents strike while a driver is preparing for a race. The majority of accidents, though, take place during racing events. Such tragedies shock and sadden onlookers and fellow competitors alike. And each accident makes racers more aware of safety.

All racing categories must follow specific safety rules. In the Unlimited class, boats must have an engine shut-off system that immediately turns off the engine if the driver is thrown from the boat.

All boats must be equipped with a white strobe light used for signaling race officials. When a boat runs into trouble—catches on fire or overturns, for instance—a driver turns on his strobe light. This shows that he is unharmed but needs help getting out of the cockpit. All boats must also have an on-board fire extinguishing system with nozzles in the cockpit.

Drivers are required to wear a life jacket, helmet, fire-retardant driving suit, and fire-retardant socks, gloves, and shoes. In addition, all drivers are examined by a doctor on the day of a race to be sure they are physically fit to compete.

In some power boat designs, the driver is not too far from the water.

RACING FLAGS

The races in each category can vary from straight drag races to closed circle races to long marathon-style races. No matter what the racing event, though, the flags used to signal the drivers always have the same meaning.

The green flag means "start" or "go." It signals competitors off the starting line at the beginning of the race. When displayed during the race, it shows that a boat is starting its final lap. The red flag means "stop"—the race has been stopped or postponed. The yellow flag means "caution," and lets drivers know that there is a hazard on the race course, such as a stopped boat. The black flag signals that all boats should leave the race course immediately. The checkered flag signals the finish line.

The drivers watch these flags very carefully. During the race, drivers can usually only see in front or to the side. They have no way of knowing what is happening behind them, and the flags keep them informed.

The flags also keep the spectators informed. The onlookers have a much more complete picture of the race than the drivers do, but they still need to know what the judges are ruling.

Whether you're a spectator or a competitor at any power boat race, you can't help but share in the excitement! The incredible spray of water behind a thunderboat, the colorful lineup of sleek machines ready to be flagged off at the starting line, the roar of finely-tuned engines, the thrill of breaking or witnessing high-speed records—these are only a few of the sights, sounds, and experiences that keep participants and fans coming back for more.

Power boat drivers love speed—and winning!

FOR MORE INFORMATION

For more information about power boat racing, its rules and regulations, and its schedule of races, write to:

American Power Boat Association
P.O. Box 377
East Detroit, MI 48021

GLOSSARY/INDEX

CATAMARAN 26 — *A boat with two side-by-side hulls.*

COUNTER ROTATION 12 — *In dual engines, a design in which the engines' propellers rotate in opposite directions. Each propeller cancels the torque produced by the other.*

DRAG 11 — *The resistance created by an object, slowing down its movement through water or air. A propeller creates an underwater drag that slows down the speed of a boat.*

DRAG RACES 14, 27, 42 — *Contests between two boats (or two other kinds of vehicles) on a straight course.*

FLATBOTTOM 18, 19, 24, 31, 34 — *A flat planing surface, with neither a tunnel (concave) or a V-shaped (convex) bottom.*

HYDROPLANE 19, 20, 21, 25, 30, 31, 34, 39 — *A hull design that causes a boat to be raised partially out of the water when moving.*

INBOARD MOTOR 9, 14, 24, 25, 26, 34, 35 — *A boat's internally mounted, nondetachable engine.*

NAVIGATOR 26, 34, 37 — *The member of a racing team in Offshore events who advises the driver which course to follow.*

GLOSSARY/INDEX

OUTBOARD MOTOR 9, 13, 14, 24, 26, 28, 30, 31 — *A boat's engine mounted or attached to the outer hull.*

PLANING SURFACE 20 — *The area of the boat that comes into contact with the water when the boat is moving.*

RUNABOUT 18, 30 — *A conventional hull with one planing surface. When the boat is racing, this planing surface is in contact with the water. A boat with one planing surface is also called a monoplane.*

SPONSONS 19, 20 — *The pontoon-like additions to the hull of a hydroplane.*

STOCK 13, 28, 30, 34 — *Any piece of boating equipment that has not been modified from its original manufactured condition.*

THROTTLEMAN 26, 34, 37 — *The member of a racing team in Offshore events who controls the throttle, giving the boat more or less power.*

TORQUE 11, 12 — *A movement in one direction produced by a boat's propeller spinning in the opposite direction.*

TURBINE 14, 15, 25, 39 — *An engine using explosive fuel to drive rotary fan blades that create the turning power of the engine. Turbine engines are commonly used in jet aircraft.*

V-BOTTOM 18, 19, 26 — *A boat's V-shaped planing surface.*